Nick Vandome

Get going with
Amazon Echo
and Alexa

WITHDRAWN

D1113051

In easy steps is an imprint of In Easy Steps Limited
16 Hamilton Terrace · Holly Walk · Leamington Spa
Warwickshire · United Kingdom · CV32 4LY
www.ineasysteps.com

Notice of Liability
Every effort has been made to ensure that this book contains accurate and
current information. However, In Easy Steps Limited and the author shall not be
liable for any loss or damage suffered by readers as a result of any information
contained herein. All prices stated in the book are correct at the time of printing.

Trademarks
All trademarks are acknowledged as belonging to their respective companies.

In Easy Steps Limited supports The Forest Stewardship Council (FSC), the leading
international forest certification organization. All our titles that are printed on
Greenpeace approved FSC certified paper carry the FSC logo.

MIX
Paper from
responsible sources
FSC® C020837

Printed and bound in the United Kingdom
ISBN 978-1-84078-814-3

Contents

1 About Echo and Alexa

Digital personal assistants are fast becoming one of the most common ways to get information and control a range of tasks in the home: from playing music to controlling a smart lighting system. One of the most popular digital personal assistants is the Amazon Echo, which is a hands-free speaker that uses Alexa to provide the voice-controlled functionality of the device. This chapter shows how to set up the Echo, using the Alexa app, so that it is ready to listen to your commands and respond to them.

About Amazon Echo

It would be nice if we could all have a personal assistant to help with day-to-day activities. Unfortunately, this is not an option for most of us, but help is at hand from the digital world. Digital personal assistants are now widely available to help with a range of tasks, from reading out the latest news to turning the lights on or off. One of the leading digital personal assistants comes from Amazon, in the form of Echo and Alexa.

The Amazon Echo is a hands-free speaker that you use to communicate with Alexa, and this is where content is delivered. Think of the Echo as the body of your digital personal assistant, and Alexa as the brains of the operation. Alexa can react to different voices, and some of the uses for the Echo and Alexa include:

- Playing music from your own music library or through an online radio station.

- Requesting the latest news and sports headlines.

- Setting up processes so that several actions can be performed in sequence.

- Making calls and sending messages to your contacts.

- Controlling smart devices in the home, including lighting systems, central heating and plugs.

The services and information delivered through the Amazon Echo by Alexa are cloud-based, which means that all of the data is stored in an Amazon computer (server) and then delivered through the Amazon Echo when it is requested. Nothing is physically stored on the Echo; it is merely a delivery system. The Echo works through connecting to your home Wi-Fi network: without Wi-Fi it will not function properly.

Models of Echo

There are several different models of Echo, which provide different functionality. This gives you the flexibility of putting different Echo models in different rooms of your home, to create the ultimate Echo experience. The models of the Echo include:

- **Echo**. Now in its 2nd generation, this is the original version of the device and can be considered as the "standard" Echo. It is a high-quality speaker that provides excellent sound for music, in addition to the full range of services from Alexa. It comes in a range of colors, and fabric covers can also be placed over the device, so that it can blend in to any room in your home. The cover style can be selected when you buy the Echo from Amazon.

Color Name: **Charcoal Fabric**

Don't forget

The standard Echo and the Echo Dot have buttons on the top of the device to control the volume, although this can also be done with voice commands to Alexa.

...cont'd

- **Echo Dot**. This is a smaller version of the standard Echo device and is a good option if you want to expand your Echo system so that you have several devices, in different rooms. If you choose to do this, each Echo can be used independently (e.g. you can play different music in the family room and a bedroom).

- **Echo Spot**. This is an Echo device that includes a circular screen, like a slightly expanded version of the Echo Dot. It provides the standard information from Alexa and it can also be used to make video calls and display movies or TV shows from a streaming service such as Amazon Video or Netflix.

Beware

The Echo Dot and the Echo Spot do not have as powerful speakers as the other Echo models, although external ones can be added with a cable or Bluetooth.

...cont'd

- **Echo Show**. This is a model of the Echo that comes with a larger screen than the Spot: 7 inches (measured diagonally). It can be used for all of the same functions as the standard Echo, plus it can be used to stream movies and TV shows and make video calls.

- **Echo Plus**. This is the largest Echo model and contains a built-in smart home hub, so it is an excellent option if you want to use it to control other Echo devices and also smart devices in the home (although much of this can also be done with the standard Echo).

The button on an Echo with a solid dot is the **Action** button. This can be used to wake up the device, enable Wi-Fi mode (if not in operation) and turn off alarms and timers.

Setting Up Amazon Echo

The Amazon Echo has to be set up for use through the Alexa app, using an Amazon account. Once this has been done you can begin exploring and using the full functionality of the Amazon Echo and Alexa.

1 Download the Amazon Alexa app to your smartphone or tablet

2 Plug in the Amazon Echo. Alexa will tell you when it is ready to be set up, via the Alexa app

3 In the Alexa app, enter your Amazon account username and password and tap on the **Sign In** button. If you do not have an Amazon account, tap on the **Create A New Amazon Account** button

○ amazon alexa

Sign in   Forgot password?

Email (phone for mobile accounts)

Amazon password

☐ Show password

SIGN IN

New to Amazon?

CREATE A NEW AMAZON ACCOUNT

4 Tap on the **Continue** button

CONTINUE

Don't forget

The Amazon Alexa app can be downloaded from the Apple App Store or the Google Play Store, or online at https://alexa.amazon.co.uk (or .com)

...cont'd

5 Tap on the **Menu** button ≡

6 Tap on the **Settings** button [Settings]

7 Tap on the **Set Up A New Device** button

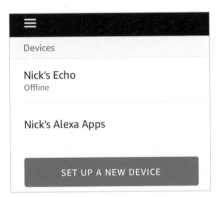

8 Tap on the required device to set up. This is also the process that is used if you want to set up additional Echo devices after the initial one has been added

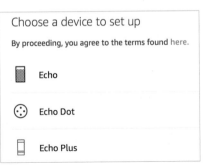

...cont'd

9 Select a language for Alexa and tap on the **Continue** button

10 Since Alexa is a cloud-based service, it needs access to the internet via your home Wi-Fi network. Tap on the **Connect To Wi-Fi** button

CONNECT TO WI-FI

11 When the light ring on the top of the Echo turns orange, tap on the **Continue** button

CONTINUE

12 In your smartphone's or tablet's Wi-Fi settings, select the **Amazon** network

13 Alexa will inform you that you have connected your Wi-Fi to the Echo and ask you to complete the setup process in the Alexa app. Tap on the **Continue** button

Connected to Echo

CONTINUE

14 Tap on your home Wi-Fi network to use this with Alexa

Select your Wi-Fi network

PlusnetWireless792287

••••••••• SHOW

Save password to Amazon
Helps connect other devices. Learn More

15 Enter your password for the Wi-Fi router

16 Tap on the **Connect** button

CONNECT

17 The Echo is prepared for use. When the **All done!** screen is displayed, tap on the **Go To Home** button to go to the Homepage of the Alexa app

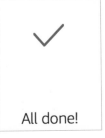

All done!

GO TO HOME

Changing the Wake Word

Each time you want to ask Alexa to do something, the wake word has to be said first to activate the Echo and Alexa. By default, the wake word is "Alexa", but this can be changed. To do this:

1 Open the Alexa app

2 Tap on the **Menu** button ☰

3 Tap on the **Settings** button `Settings`

4 Tap on your Echo's name; e.g. Nick's Echo (make sure it is showing **Online**)

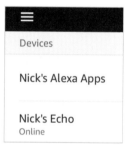

☰
Devices
Nick's Alexa Apps
Nick's Echo Online

5 Tap on the **Wake Word** button

> Wake Word
> Alexa

The Echo name can be changed by selecting **Alexa app** > **Menu** > **Settings** > **Device name** > **Edit,** tapping on the existing name and entering a new one.

6 Tap on the down-pointing arrow next to
Alexa Device wake word

Alexa Device wake word:

Alexa

SAVE

7 Select a new wake word

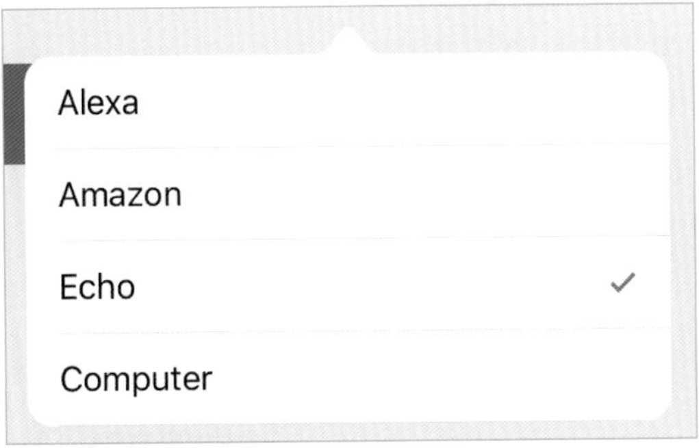

Alexa

Amazon

Echo ✓

Computer

8 Tap on the **Save** button to apply the new wake word for
activating Alexa

SAVE

Changing Alexa's Accent

The voice used on the Echo cannot be changed from a female one, but the accent can be changed. To do this:

1 Open the Alexa app and access **Menu** > **Settings** > **Echo name**, as shown on page 14

2 Tap on the **Language** button

Language	English (United States) >

3 Tap on the down-pointing arrow next to the existing language

Change Alexa's Language

English (United States) ⌄

4 Select a new language (this will be the accent used by Alexa)

Deutsch

English (United States)

English (Canada)

English (India)

English (Australia)

English (United Kingdom) ✓

日本語

5 Tap on the **Save Changes** button to apply the new language and accent for Alexa

SAVE CHANGES

Setting Your Location

It is important that Alexa knows your location (or more accurately, the location of your Amazon Echo) so that specific items can be tailored to it; i.e. when you ask for the current weather, or restaurant recommendations nearby. To set your location:

1 Open the Alexa app and access **Menu** > **Settings** > **Echo name**, as shown on page 14

2 Tap on the **Edit** button next to **Device location**

Device location
This location will be used for weather, time zone and other local features.
→Edit

3 Enter a location for the Amazon Echo and tap on the **Save** button

Device location
This location will be used for weather, time zone and other local features.

United Kingdom

EH1 1AB

Edinburgh

21 High Street

Apartment, suite, unit, building, floor, etc.

State/Province/Region

SAVE

4 The location entered in Step 3 is displayed under the **Device location** heading and this will be used by Alexa

Device location
This location will be used for weather, time zone and other local features.

21 High Street, Edinburgh, GB EH1 1AB

Around Alexa's Home

Within the Alexa app, the Homepage can be used to display the requests that have been made of Alexa and also give feedback about the accuracy of voice commands that have been made.

1 Open the Alexa app and tap on this icon at the bottom of the screen to view the Homepage

2 The top panel offers suggestions for questions to ask Alexa

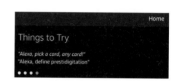

3 The results for voice commands that have been made are shown below the top panel, with the most recent one at the top

4 Tap on the **More** button to provide voice feedback

5 Tap on the **Yes** or **No** buttons to provide feedback

about whether Alexa heard your command correctly. This is used to train Alexa for subsequent requests

2 Asking Alexa

This chapter shows how to start asking Alexa questions, whether it is specific commands or general queries that do not have a definitive answer. It also deals with specifying which items appear in the Flash Briefing, which is a daily news update that can include news bulletins from various outlets. The chapter also covers getting the latest news for your favorite sports teams, and selecting traffic routes so that Alexa can update you about any problems and also the quickest route to take.

Getting Started with Alexa

Once the Echo and Alexa have been set up you can start making requests of Alexa. Each request has to begin with "Alexa...:" (or the wake word you have chosen), otherwise you will be met with a stony silence. Some simple questions to ask Alexa to begin with include:

- "Alexa, what time is it?".

- "Alexa, what is the current weather?" (This is based on the location of the Echo, as shown on page 17.)

- "Alexa, will it rain tomorrow?".

- "Alexa, play radio station XXX". (Alexa will play the requested radio station as long as it is available on TuneIn, which is the radio player for the Echo and Alexa.)

- "Alexa, play [selected music or artist]". (This is taken from any music that you have in your Amazon Music Library that has either been bought from Amazon, or streamed from a streaming service.)

- "Alexa, stop".

- "Alexa, pause".

- "Alexa, volume up/down" or "Alexa, volume [1-10]".

- "Alexa, tell me a joke".

- "Alexa, set a timer for XX minutes".

- "Alexa, what is the definition of [selected word]?".

...cont'd

- "Alexa, tell me the news". (This can be customized with different news providers; see pages 24-25 for details.)

- "Alexa, how do you say [selected word] in [selected language]?".

- "Alexa, what is the square root of 81?".

- "Alexa, what is the capital of [country]?".

- "Alexa, what movies are playing nearby?". (This is based on the location for the Echo, as shown on page 17.)

- "Alexa, list Italian restaurants nearby". (As above.)

- "Alexa, help" – to get details of the type of help questions that can be asked; e.g. "Alexa, how do I connect to Bluetooth?".

- "Alexa, how many kilometers in a mile?".

- "Alexa, how many grams in an ounce?".

- "Alexa, how many US dollars to the UK pound?".

- "Alexa, give me a recipe for [selected dish]".

- "Alexa, give me a tip".

Beware

If you are playing music, or a radio station, Alexa will return to it after you ask a question such as "Alexa, what is the time?", but not after an item such as a news briefing.

Asking Alexa's Opinion

In addition to asking Alexa to perform specific tasks, such as playing a song or answering a factual question, you can also ask Alexa a range of questions that require an opinion. This may not always result in the expected answer, or any answer at all, but it can be fun asking Alexa a selection of random questions. Some to try include:

- "Alexa, how are you?".

- "Alexa, am I good-looking?".

- "Alexa, do you like me?".

- "Alexa, what do you look like?".

- "Alexa, how old are you?".

- "Alexa, what's the meaning of life?".

- "Alexa, what's your favorite tablet?".

- "Alexa, what do you eat?".

- "Alexa, what's your favorite movie?". (Alexa can be a bit fickle and if you ask this several times you may get a different answer each time. Similarly, when asking Alexa about items such as favorite song, book, TV show or opera.)

Don't forget

If you ask Alexa a question such as, "Alexa, what is the best movie of all time?", the answer will be based on information from the web, such as movie details from IMDb.

Viewing Details from the App

For some questions, Alexa is able to give a simple, definitive answer. However, for other questions more information about the answer can be viewed on Wikipedia, or other online services connected to the answer, through the Alexa app. To do this:

1 Open the Alexa app and tap on the Homepage icon

2 The result for the most recent item is displayed at the top of the Homepage. If there is additional information available from Wikipedia, tap on the **Wikipedia** link

Describe the color blue

Image: Wikipedia

Blue is one of the three primary colours of pigments in painting and traditional colour theory, as well as in the RGB colour model.

LEARN MORE ON WIKIPEDIA

3 For items such as restaurants nearby, or movies playing nearby, tap on one of the results to view its details

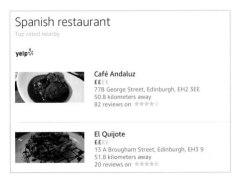

Spanish restaurant
Top rated nearby

yelp

Café Andaluz
££££
77B George Street, Edinburgh, EH2 3EE
50.8 kilometres away
82 reviews on ★★★★☆

El Quijote
££££
13 A Brougham Street, Edinburgh, EH3 9
51.8 kilometres away
20 reviews on ★★★★☆

Keeping Up with the News

Alexa is an excellent option for keeping up with the daily news and you can request a news update at any time, simply by saying, "Alexa, what's the news?". This will result in a news briefing that is taken from a specific online news service. It is possible to customize this so that your news comes from one, or more, of your favorite news outlets. To do this:

1 Open the Alexa app and access **Menu** > **Settings**

2 Tap on the **Flash Briefing** button   Flash Briefing

3 Drag the buttons On or Off for the Flash Briefing items

Flash Briefing	Edit Order
Get more Flash Briefing content	>
On	
Headlines from BBC News BBC News	⬤
Today's Forecast Weather	⬤

4 Tap on the **Get more Flash Briefing content** button

If you say, "Alexa, play Flash Briefing", updates from all of the selected items will be included; e.g. news, weather and sport.

5 Tap on an item you want included in the Flash Briefing

6 Tap on the **Enable** button to include the item

7 The item is included in the Flash Briefing list. Drag its button On or Off to include or exclude it from the Flash Briefing

If you say, "Alexa, what's the news?" you will get the whole of the Flash Briefing, not just the news items.

Editing the Flash Briefing

Within the Flash Briefing it is possible to change the order in which items appear. To do this:

1 Open the Alexa app and access **Menu** > **Settings**

2 Tap on the **Flash Briefing** button   Flash Briefing

3 Tap on the **Edit Order** button

Edit Order

4 Drag on these buttons to change the order in which the items will appear in the Flash Briefing, and tap on the **Done** button   Done

Receiving Sports Updates

Delivering the latest sports news is another speciality of Alexa, and it is possible to customize this for your favorite sports teams. To do this:

1 Open the Alexa app and access **Menu** > **Settings**

2 Tap on the **Sports Update** button | Sports Update |

3 Enter a team name in the Search box and tap on one of the options to add it to the list of teams that will be included in the sports update

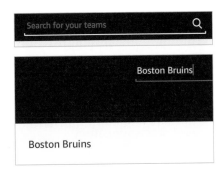

4 Results from each included team will be covered sequentially when you ask, "Alexa,

what's the sports news?". Each update will include the latest result for each team and also their next fixture. Tap on a cross next to a team to remove it from the list for sports updates

Beating the Traffic

Alexa can be used to provide traffic information between two points, so that you can plan your journey accordingly. This can be done as a one-off between two locations, or you can apply traffic settings for your daily commute, from your home to your place of work.

1 Open the Alexa app and access **Menu** > **Settings**

2 Tap on the **Traffic** button Traffic

3 By default, the **From** location is your home location that is determined under **Settings** > **[My Echo name]** > **Device location**

4 Tap on the **Change address** button to change the **From** address

Change address

5 Enter a new address and tap on the **Save Changes** button

...cont'd

6 Tap on the **Add address** button and select an address in the same way as for the From address

Traffic
Enter location information for your traffic update
○ From **25 High Street, Edinburgh Scotland EH1 1** Change address
Add stop
○ To Add address

To
Add address

7 When you ask Alexa, "Alexa, what's the traffic?" the reply will include traffic information between the two locations in the Traffic setting, and also the fastest route to take. Access the Alexa app to view details of the route, although this does not have step-by-step instructions

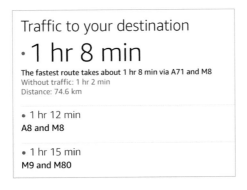

Traffic to your destination
· 1 hr 8 min
The fastest route takes about 1 hr 8 min via A71 and M8
Without traffic: 1 hr 2 min
Distance: 74.6 km

• 1 hr 12 min
A8 and M8

• 1 hr 15 min
M9 and M80

Settings for Alexa

Within the Alexa app it is possible to change a range of settings for how Alexa operates. To do this:

1 Open the Alexa app and access **Menu** > **Settings**

2 Tap on the **Alexa Apps** button

Nick's Alexa Apps

3 Select a location and time for Alexa to use to tailor items such as weather forecasts

Nick's Alexa Apps

Device location
This location will be used for weather, time zone and other local features.

Add a street address for better local information.
No ZIP code set

Device time zone

Select a Region

4 Drag these buttons On or Off to enable, or disable, metric measurements to be used as the unit of temperature and distance by Alexa

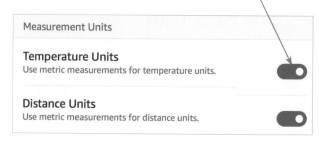

Measurement Units

Temperature Units
Use metric measurements for temperature units.

Distance Units
Use metric measurements for distance units.

3 Alexa Skills

Much of Alexa's functionality is achieved through skills: services that are similar to using apps on a smartphone or tablet. This chapter shows how to get started with Alexa's skills and start adding to the pre-installed ones, so that you can provide Alexa with exactly the skills that you require. It also covers managing and using Alexa's skills and, where required, linking them to online services to increase their functionality.

About Skills

The functionality of Alexa (i.e. the tasks that it can perform) is known as "skills". This is similar to using an app on a smartphone or a tablet. Some skills are already pre-installed for Alexa, while others can be added to increase Alexa's functionality. For instance, providing the time and date is a pre-installed skill, while managing a calendar is a skill that can be added. To start using skills with Alexa:

1 Open the Alexa app and tap on the **Menu** button

2 Tap on the **Skills** button Skills

3 The Skills page is displayed. The top panel contains featured skills, with individual skills listed below

...cont'd

4 Swipe up and down the page to view all of the available skills

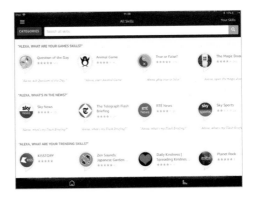

5 Tap on the **Categories** button at the top of the window

CATEGORIES

6 Tap on a category to view skills for specific areas. Tap in the **Search all skills** box to search using keywords over all of the available skills

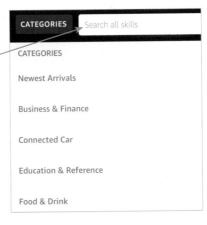

Viewing Your Skills

It is possible to view all of the skills to which Alexa has access, including the pre-installed ones and those that have been added:

1 Open the Alexa app and access **Menu** > **Skills**

2 Tap on the **Your Skills** button in the top right-hand corner of the Skills window

Your Skills

3 The **Your Skills** window is where you can manage the skills used by Alexa. Tap on the **Recently Added** tab to view the most recently added skills

4 Tap on the **All Skills** tab to view all of the skills currently available to Alexa

ALL SKILLS

5   Tap on the **Needs Attention** tab to view skills that require an action

taken, such as linking them to an online account

6   Tap on the **All Skills** button or the **Find More Skills** button to return to the main Skills window, from where more skills can be added

7   Tap on a skill in the main window to view details about it. Tap on the **Disable Skill** button to turn off the skill so that it is not available to Alexa. Tap on the **Settings** button to view its settings

Some pre-installed skills cannot be disabled (e.g. the time and date), and these do not appear in the list of skills.

Adding Skills

Several skills can be added for Alexa, to increase the overall functionality of the system. To do this:

1 Open the Alexa app and access **Menu** > **Skills**

2 Tap on a skill in the main Skills window, or search for one using the **Categories** button or the **Search** box at the top of the window

3 For the selected skill, tap on the **Enable** button, above a description of the skill

...cont'd

4 The skill is added to the Skills window, under the **Recently Added** and **All Skills** tabs in the **Your Skills** section. The number of currently enabled skills is also displayed

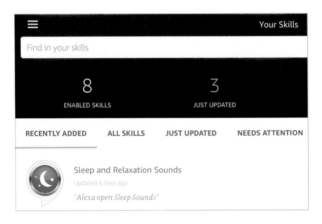

5 To disable a skill, access the **Your Skills** window and tap on the **Disable Skill** button. Once a skill has been disabled it can be enabled again, using the same process that was used to enable it initially

News and sports skills can be added from different media providers. These can then be included in the Flash Briefing news update.

37

Using Skills

Because of the range of skills available for Alexa, there is no definitive way to use them. However, a good starting point can be to ask Alexa about a specific skill. For instance, if you are using the Sleep Sounds skill you can ask Alexa for details about it, such as:

● "Alexa, tell me about Sleep Sounds."

When using a skill it is sometimes necessary to ask Alexa to access the skill and then request an item within it:

● "Alexa, ask Sleep Sounds to play City Rain."

Details about a skill can also be viewed on the Homepage of the Alexa app. For instance, you can ask Alexa to list the sounds within the Sleep Sounds skill, and these are listed within the Alexa app too:

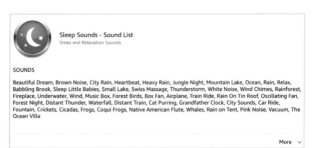

Sleep Sounds - Sound List
Sleep and Relaxation Sounds

SOUNDS

Beautiful Dream, Brown Noise, City Rain, Heartbeat, Heavy Rain, Jungle Night, Mountain Lake, Ocean, Rain, Relax, Babbling Brook, Sleep Little Babies, Small Lake, Swiss Massage, Thunderstorm, White Noise, Wind Chimes, Rainforest, Fireplace, Underwater, Wind, Music Box, Forest Birds, Box Fan, Airplane, Train Ride, Rain On Tin Roof, Oscillating Fan, Forest Night, Distant Thunder, Waterfall, Distant Train, Cat Purring, Grandfather Clock, City Sounds, Car Ride, Fountain, Crickets, Cicadas, Frogs, Coqui Frogs, Native American Flute, Whales, Rain on Tent, Pink Noise, Vacuum, The Ocean Villa

More ⌄

Beware

Alexa takes requests literally, so if you say "Alexa, play Wind", the result may be a song of that title from Amazon. For a specific item say, "Alexa, ask [skill name] to play Wind".

Linking Skills

Some skills need to be linked to an online account in order for them to work properly. This is usually when the skill is connected to an app that is linked to a specific account, in order to deliver its services. To link a skill for use with Alexa:

1 In the Alexa app a skill requiring a linked account is indicated below the **Enable** button, with the words **Account linking required**

2 Tap on the **Enable** button. If the skill is connected to content in the Amazon cloud, the skill is linked by signing in with your Amazon account details

3 If the skill is linked to an independent service, such as the Philips Hue smart lighting system, the sign-in details will be the ones used when the service was first set up. A new account can also be created, if there is not one in place

Some Skills to Try

Some useful and fun skills to get started with include:

Cookery
Healthy Meals. This can be used to provide random healthy meal ideas. Ask Alexa, "Alexa, ask Healthy Meals for a recipe".

Shopping
Bring! Shopping list (linked account required). Use this to create shopping lists that can be added to by other family members. Say to Alexa, "Alexa, open Bring and add apples".

Relaxation
Zen Sounds: Japanese Garden Sounds. Use this skill to play a range of relaxing sounds. Ask Alexa, "Alexa, open Japanese Garden Sounds".

Health and Fitness
7-Minute Workout. Keep fit with Alexa with this skill for performing a short workout. Ask Alexa, "Alexa, start 7-Minute Workout".

Games
Word Tennis. This is a word game you can play with Alexa. Alexa starts with a category and then words have to be chosen from this category. Ask Alexa, "Alexa, play Word Tennis".

Reference
Wiki Brains. Check up on various facts with this Wiki-related skill. Ask Alexa, "Alexa, ask Wiki Brains about digital voice assistants".

Miscellaneous
Random facts. A fun skill – Alexa will provide you with a range of interesting facts. Ask Alexa, "Alexa, give me a random fact".

4 Getting Organized

Alexa can be used for a range of organizational tasks, from creating lists to reading entries on your calendar. This chapter shows how to set up Alexa's organizational options including: linking Alexa to list apps for creating lists, which can be added to via Alexa; adding online calendars that can be accessed by Alexa; and creating routines, which are a sequence of commands that are actioned by Alexa when a trigger word or phrase is used, or at a specific time.

Starting with Lists

Alexa can be used to create numerous lists, either for to-do items or shopping lists. To do this, Alexa has to be given the means to create and read lists. To do this:

1 Open the Alexa app and access **Menu > Settings**

2 Tap on the **Lists** button   Lists

3 Tap on the **Get Skill** button next to an item to use this as the default list creator for Alexa

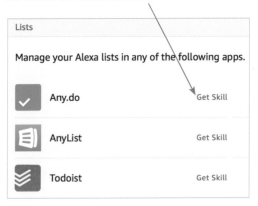

More list options can be found in the Alexa app under **Menu > Skills**. Enter "lists" into the Search box at the top of the window to view the results.

4 Details of the item are listed. Tap on the **Enable** button to allow Alexa to use it

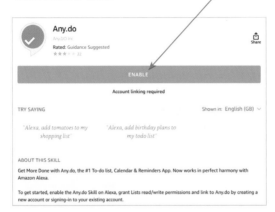

5 Give the list the required permissions by dragging these buttons On or Off, and tap on **Save Permissions**

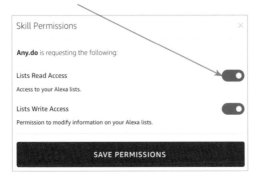

43

Linking List Accounts

Once a list skill has been added for Alexa you usually need to create an account, so that list items added via Alexa are also included in the same lists on other devices. For instance, if you have the Any.do list app on your smartphone or tablet, this can be linked to lists used by Alexa. To do this:

1 Once the list skill has been added to Alexa, tap on one of the options for creating an account via the Alexa app. This can be done with details from a Facebook account or a Google account or with an email address and password

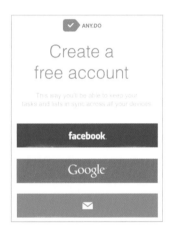

2 Enter the login details for the selected method and tap on the **Create Account** button

3 If the list has been successfully linked to Alexa, this is displayed on a notification page. Tap on the **Done** button

4 For some list options, the list app has to be downloaded to a smartphone or tablet from the related app store, and the account created through the app. The sign-in details can then be used in the Alexa skill to link the list account

Adding Items to Lists

Lists used by Alexa usually consist of to-do lists or shopping lists. For each one it is best to specify a list for an item, such as, "Alexa, add milk to my shopping list", or "Alexa, add pick up dry cleaning to my to-do list". However, Alexa will also generally recognize the type of item that is being requested and add it to the correct list by default.

Once a list has been created it can be accessed in two ways:

1 Ask Alexa, "Alexa, what is on my shopping/to-do list?" and the items will be narrated

2 Access the list app on a smartphone or tablet to view the items that have been added. The items added via Alexa are displayed within their own list (other lists can be added within the app)

Any.do

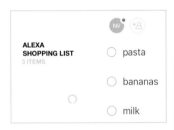

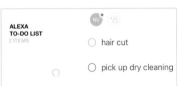

If a list skill is disabled on Alexa, the Alexa lists will also be disabled on the related list app.

Adding a Calendar

Alexa can use calendars for adding events and telling you about upcoming appointments. Online calendars such as those stored in iCloud for iPhone and iPad users, Microsoft or Google can be used with Alexa. To use these, they have to be first set up with the Alexa app:

1 Open the Alexa app and access **Menu** > **Settings**

2 Tap on the **Calendar** button Calendar

3 Tap on the online calendar that you want to add

Calendars

G **Google** (0 linked accounts)
Gmail & G Suite

Microsoft (0 linked accounts)
Outlook.com & Office 365

Apple (0 linked accounts)
iCloud

Alexa will add new events to this calendar:

It is best to just use one online calendar, otherwise you may end up having to duplicate events and this could cause confusion for Alexa.

Hot tip

...cont'd

4 Tap on the **Link this [account name] account** button

Nick Vandome

Link this Google account

5 Enter the login details for the selected account (email address and password) and tap on the **Next** button after each item

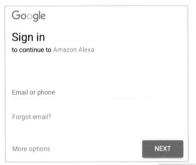

Google

Sign in
to continue to Amazon Alexa

Email or phone

Forgot email?

More options   NEXT

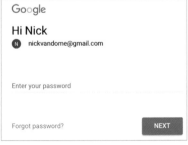

Google

Hi Nick
🅝 nickvandome@gmail.com

Enter your password

Forgot password?   NEXT

...cont'd

6
Tap on the **Allow** button to enable Alexa to manage the calendar in the selected account

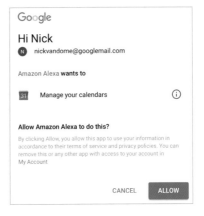

Google

Hi Nick
N nickvandome@googlemail.com

Amazon Alexa **wants to**

31 Manage your calendars   ⓘ

Allow Amazon Alexa to do this?

By clicking Allow, you allow this app to use your information in accordance to their terms of service and privacy policies. You can remove this or any other app with access to your account in My Account

                              CANCEL   **ALLOW**

49

7
Tap on the **Done** button to complete the setup process

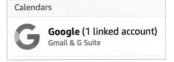

Done <   >   layla.amazon.com

Done.
Alexa is now ready to use your Google calendar. You can now return to your Alexa app.

8
The account shows as **linked** in the Calendars section of Settings within the Alexa app

Calendars

G **Google** (1 linked account)
Gmail & G Suite

If you are using an iCloud calendar for an iPhone or iPad, you will be asked to set up two-factor authentication on your device before you can add the calendar.

Using Calendars

Once a calendar has been linked to Alexa, you can start using Alexa to add calendar events and for asking about items that are in your calendar:

1 Alexa is quite flexible in terms of calendar requests. For instance, you can say, "Alexa, what's my next appointment?", or, "Alexa, what do I have on this week?". For the latter, Alexa will narrate all of the events that are in your calendar for the current week (or time period, as specified)

2 To add a calendar event, say to Alexa, "Alexa, add event for tomorrow at 10 am, play tennis"

3 The event is added to the calendar and also displayed in the Alexa app. This will be narrated by Alexa if you ask for an appointment on this date

---

Event Created

10:00 AM | **Play tennis**
2/20/2018
10:00 AM—11:00 AM
Google: Nick Vandome/ nickvandome@gmail.com

Delete event

Don't forget

If you want to add an event at 12 o'clock, Alexa will ask you if you mean 12 o'clock in the morning or the evening.

Creating Routines

Alexa is definitely not a one-trick pony, and can remember a series of commands as a sequence and action them with a single trigger word or phrase. This is known as a routine and is an excellent option if you regularly perform the same sequence of events; e.g. listen to the news, get the latest traffic update, or the current weather.

To create routines with Alexa:

1   Open the Alexa app and tap on the **Menu** button

2   Tap on the **Routines** button   Routines

3   Tap on the **Create Routine** button

4   Tap on the **When this happens** button to select a trigger word or phrase for the routine

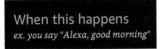

5   Select whether the routine is triggered by a word or phrase, or at a specific time

...cont'd

6 For the **When you say something** option, enter the word or phrase that will trigger the routine

7 Tap on the **Save** button at the bottom of the screen

SAVE

8 Tap on the **Add action** button

Add action

9 Tap on one of the options for the first action of the routine. These include options for Alexa speaking a phrase, reading a Flash Briefing, operating a smart home device, giving a traffic update or a weather forecast

...cont'd

10. The selected item is displayed. Tap on the **Add** button to include it in the routine

Alexa will play the news from your Flash Briefing
ADD

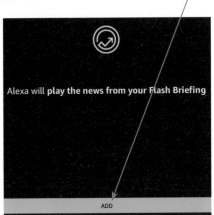

11. The action is added to the current routine

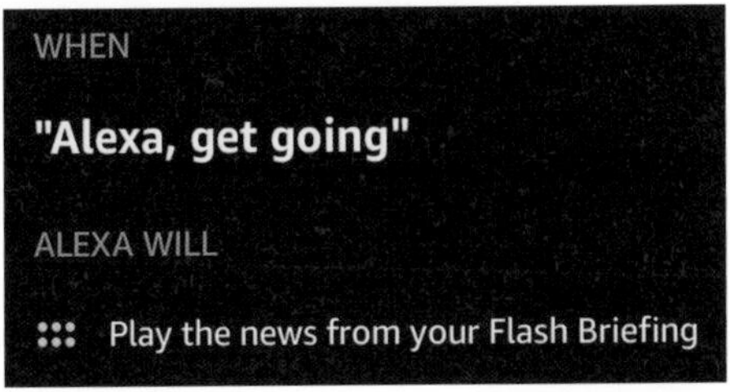

WHEN
"Alexa, get going"
ALEXA WILL
Play the news from your Flash Briefing

12. Tap on the **Add action** button to add more actions to the current routine

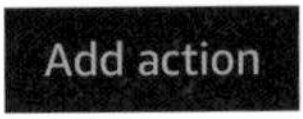

Add action

...cont'd

13 All of the actions will be played when the trigger word or phrase is spoken

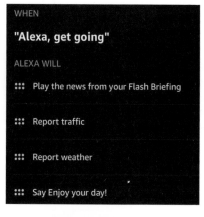

WHEN

"Alexa, get going"

ALEXA WILL

⋮⋮⋮ Play the news from your Flash Briefing

⋮⋮⋮ Report traffic

⋮⋮⋮ Report weather

⋮⋮⋮ Say Enjoy your day!

14 Tap on the **Create** button to create the routine

CREATE

15 To add another routine, tap on the **+** button in the top right-hand corner of the **Routines** Homepage within the Settings section of the Alexa app

16 For the **At scheduled time** routine option, tap on the **At Time** and **Repeat** buttons to select a time and day for the routine, and select actions in the same way as for the **When you say something** option

At Time

Repeat

5 Voice Calls and Messages

The Echo and Alexa can do a lot more than answering questions and keeping you up-to-date with the latest news and weather. If linked to your smartphone and the Alexa app, you can use the Echo to send and receive voice and text messages. This chapter shows how to set up your smartphone for voice calls and text messages with Alexa, and details sending and receiving each type of message. This results in developing your Echo as an effective two-way communication device that you can contact remotely, from a smartphone.

Setting Up Voice Calling

Smartphones are frequently used for hands-free voice calls. Alexa can also get in on the act of voice calls, and messaging, between two Echo users, provided that both of them have been set up for this. To do this on your own Echo:

1 Download the Alexa app to your smartphone and tap on it to open it

2 Tap on your own name to let Alexa know that voice calls and messaging will come from you

3 Enter the name that you want to be displayed when you make a voice call or send a message via Alexa

4 Tap on the **Continue** button

5   Tap on the **Allow** button to enable Amazon to upload your contacts to help Alexa with making calls and messaging, and also sending notifications. This is optional (see next page about adding contacts for Alexa to use)

6   Enter a smartphone number that will be used by Alexa for accessing your contacts. Tap on the **Continue** button

7   A verification code will be sent to the number entered in Step 6. Enter the verification code and tap on the **Continue** button to finish the setup process for voice calling and messaging with Alexa

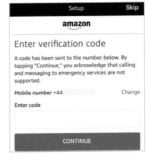

Adding Contacts to Alexa

In order to make voice calls and send messages, Alexa must have access to the contacts on your smartphone. To enable this:

1 Access the Amazon Alexa option within the Settings on your smartphone

2 Drag the **Contacts** button to On to allow Alexa to have access to your contacts

3 To make voice calls and send messages to another Echo user, they must have their contact list enabled for the Alexa app and also have performed the setup process on the pages 56-57

Text messages are sent to the Alexa app on the recipient's smartphone, rather than their standard messaging app.

Calling from Alexa

After voice calling and messaging have been set up, you can use Alexa to call and message other people who have an Echo and have also set it up for these functions. To make a call to someone in this way:

1 Say, "Alexa, call Nick". Alexa will repeat the recipient's name to ensure that you have the correct person

2 The call is made to the recipient's smartphone, via the Alexa app, rather than the regular phone app

3 The recipient taps on the **Accept** button to take the call. Whatever is spoken to the Echo will be heard on the recipient's smartphone, via the Alexa app

If music is playing when a call is made to Alexa it may need to be paused before the call is taken, otherwise it could continue in the background at the same time.

Calling to Alexa

If you are away from home you can call Alexa from the Alexa app on your smartphone. To do this:

1 Open the Alexa app and tap on the **Conversations** button on the bottom toolbar

2 Tap on this button at the top of the window to access available contacts

3 Tap on the required contact

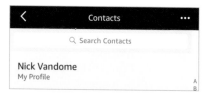

4 Tap on this button to make a call to the contact, via their Echo and Alexa. (Use the Video button to make a video call to an Echo Show)

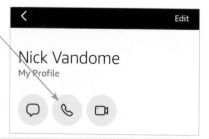

If a contact has set up their Echo for voice calls and messaging, their name will be in bold in the contacts list.

Messaging from Alexa

To send a text message from Alexa to another Echo user:

1 Say, "Alexa, send a message to Nick". Alexa will ask what message you want to send. Tell Alexa the required message (you do not have to precede this with "Alexa")

2 The message is sent to the recipient's Alexa app on their smartphone. The message is accessed from the **Conversations** button on the bottom toolbar. If there are new messages this will be indicated by a green dot on the icon

3 The latest message is shown at the top of the Conversations window. The number of unread messages in each conversation is shown here

≡	Conversations	人	☑
Nick Vandome			11:11
Hello nick			**1**

4 Tap on the message to reply to it. Tap on the microphone

icon to send a voice reply, or tap on the keyboard icon to send a text message reply. The reply will be sent to Alexa on the original sender's Echo

Messaging to Alexa

Using the Alexa app it is possible to send a text message to your own Echo, or to another Echo user who has this set up. To do this:

1. Open the Alexa app and tap on the **Conversations** button on the bottom toolbar

2. Tap on this button at the top of the window to access available contacts

3. Tap on the required contact

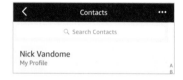

4. Tap on this button to create a text message to the contact's Echo

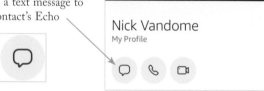

5. Compose the message and tap on this button to send

it. Once a message has been sent to an Echo a notification sound is played and the message can be heard by saying, "Alexa, what are my messages?"

6 Music

Listening to music has been revolutionized by digital devices, and this is continued with the Echo and Alexa. This chapter looks at how to use the Amazon website to access a wide range of music in different ways: from buying individual tracks and albums to potentially streaming millions of songs using the Amazon Music Unlimited subscription service. It also covers how to link to music services using the Alexa app and shows how you can start listening to radio stations from around the world.

Music Options

One of the most common uses for the Echo is playing music. The standard Echo and the Echo Plus are excellent for this since they have high-quality speakers. There are several options for the way you can access music on an Echo:

- Buy specific tracks or albums of music from Amazon and play them from your Amazon Music Library. Music that is obtained this way can also be played on a range of devices, including PC, Mac, smartphone and tablet (iOS and Android).

- Subscribe to Amazon Music Unlimited and stream it to your Echo.

- Link to another music subscription service, such as Spotify.

- Listen to radio stations, using the TuneIn radio service.

- It is also possible to stream music from an Echo to a connected device; i.e. a Bluetooth speaker.

When playing music, Alexa can perform a range of tasks, such as:

- "Alexa, play [album] by [artist]".

- "Alexa, play next/previous song" (if an album is being played).

- "Alexa, play [song name] by [artist]".

- "Alexa, pause/stop song".

- "Alexa, play songs with Rain in the title".

Buying Music from Amazon

Music can be bought from the Amazon website and then accessed in a variety of ways, including via Alexa. It can also be played on a smartphone or tablet using the Amazon Music app. To use music from the Amazon website:

1 Access the Amazon website and search for an item of music or access it within the Amazon Music **Download Store** section

2 Access the required track or album and tap on the **MP3** option to download a digital version of the item

3 To view items that you have downloaded, click on the **Your Account** button at the right-hand side of the top toolbar and click on the **Your Music** button

Playing Amazon Music

Music that has been downloaded from the Amazon Music Download Store is saved to your Amazon Music Library and it can be played in a number of ways from here:

- Access the **Your Music** section on the Amazon website, as shown on the previous page, and click on the item that you want to play.

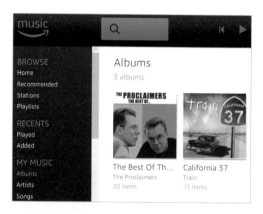

- Download the **Amazon Music** app to an iOS or Android smartphone or tablet and access your Amazon Music Library from here.

- Ask Alexa to play an item from your Amazon Music Library, using one of the commands on page 64.

The items available to Alexa will be the same as in the Amazon Music app. For a greater range of music, subscribe to an online streaming service (see next four pages).

Amazon Music Unlimited

If you want to expand the music repertoire that is available to be played by Alexa, the Amazon Music Unlimited service is a good place to start. This is a paid-for streaming service, but it gives you access to the full library of music on Amazon (over 40 million songs). The full service can be used for a variety of devices, but there is also an Echo-specific service that is cheaper than the full version. To use this:

1. On the Amazon website Homepage click on the **Music** option. (If this is not showing, enter **Music Unlimited Echo** into the Search box)

2. Details about the Music Unlimited option are displayed. This can be accessed directly through Alexa by saying, "Alexa, try Amazon Music Unlimited". (There is a 30-day free trial, as there is for the full Music Unlimited service)

The Music Unlimited Echo subscription is £3.99 (UK)/$3.99 (US). There are also individual and family options for the full service (reduced for Amazon Prime members).

Amazon Prime Music

The Amazon Prime subscription service includes a range of benefits, such as free one-day delivery on qualifying purchases; free streaming of movies and TV shows; and Kindle books. It also offers access to Prime Music, which contains over two million songs that can be accessed and played by Alexa. Amazon Prime is a subscription service that costs £79 UK/$99 US for a year. There is also a 30-day free trial.

1 On the Amazon website Homepage click on the **Try Prime** option, or

2 Enter **Prime Music** into the Search box on the Amazon website Homepage to view details about this service

3 Click on the **Start your 30-day Prime free trial** button to begin using Prime. (To cancel, click on **Your Account** on the top toolbar and click on the **Your Prime Membership** button and the **End Membership and Benefits** button)

If you have a Music Unlimited or Prime Music subscription, Alexa will be able to conduct a wider range of music-related commands due to the amount of available music.

Hot tip

Subscribing Through Alexa

In addition to using music directly from the Amazon website, it is also possible to connect to music streaming services through the Alexa app:

1 Open the Alexa app and access **Menu** > **Settings**

2 Tap on the **Music & Media** button   Music & Media

3 The current music services are listed

4 Tap on an item to sign up for the streaming service, or link to it if you already have an account with the service, such as Spotify

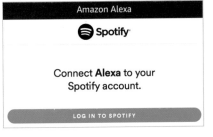

...cont'd

Selecting a default account

If you have linked to more than one music streaming service, which is perfectly possible, a default one has to be specified. This will be the music library that Alexa will look in first when you make a request for playing an item of music. To specify a default music account:

1 Access the Music & Media section of the Settings within the Alexa app, as shown on page 69, and tap on the **Choose Default Music Services** button

CHOOSE DEFAULT MUSIC SERVICES

2 Tap on a music service to select it as the default music library and tap on the **Done** button

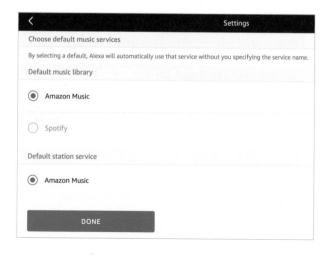

Listening to the Radio

For radio lovers, Alexa uses the TuneIn radio service to provide a huge range of local, national and international radio stations, covering music, talk radio, sports and news.

1 Say, "Alexa, play radio Country 104". Open the Alexa app. At the top of the Homepage is the currently playing radio station from TuneIn

2 Tap on the **Browse TuneIn** button to view all of the available stations

BROWSE TUNEIN

3 The Search page can be used to search for specific items in the **Search TuneIn** Search box at the top of the page, or items can be browsed for from the category headings

Some radio stations can be accessed by saying, "Alexa, play..." followed by the station name. However, some require the word "radio" before the station name.

Beware

...cont'd

4 Tap on a sub-category within the main category to view the available stations within this criteria

5 Tap on a station to start playing it via your Echo. This will replace any previously playing radio station. The currently playing song is displayed underneath the station name

All radio stations that have been played appear on the timeline of items on the Alexa app Homepage. This can be a good way to access previously played stations.

Pairing Bluetooth Speakers

The Echo is very versatile and can, in addition to being used as a speaker in its own right, be linked to an external Bluetooth speaker, so this can be used as an output device for Alexa commands and responses. This has to be with a separate Bluetooth device that has to be "paired" with the Echo so that the two devices can communicate with each other. This is done through the Alexa app:

1 Open the Alexa app and access **Menu** > **Settings**

2 Tap on your Echo's name

> Nick's Echo
> Online

3 Tap on the **Pair Alexa Gadget** button (the Bluetooth device has to be in pairing mode – consult the user instructions for details about accessing this mode)

> Pair Alexa Gadget

4 Tap on the device to be paired. Once this is done, all of the output from the Echo will play through this device

> Available Devices
>
> Please make sure your device is in pairing mode.
>
> • • •
>
> SoundCore mini

Beware

If the output from the Echo is being played through a connected Bluetooth speaker, the Echo cannot be used separately for different content.

Managing Bluetooth Devices

Different Bluetooth devices can be paired with an Echo, and they can be managed using the Alexa app:

1 Open the Alexa app and access **Menu** > **Settings**

2 Tap on the **Bluetooth** button

Bluetooth

3 Items that have been paired are listed under the **Bluetooth Devices** heading

Bluetooth Devices

Select a previously paired device

※ SoundCore mini ⌄

4 Tap on the down-pointing arrow next to a device to access options for managing it. Tap on the **Disconnect** button to disconnect the current session. Tap on the **Forget**

Bluetooth Devices

Select a previously paired device

※ SoundCore mini ⌃

Disconnect

Forget Device

Device button to unpair the device. It will need to be paired again if you want to use it with your Echo

7 Shopping

Amazon is one of the major online retailers on the web. Using your Echo and Alexa you can make use of this valuable resource and order eligible items using voice purchasing by asking Alexa. This chapter shows you how to set up voice purchasing and link to 1-Click purchasing through your Amazon account. It also details the types of items that can be ordered with voice purchasing, and some of the commands that can be used with Alexa to achieve this.

Setting Up Voice Purchasing

The Echo can be used to buy items from the Amazon website, with its voice purchasing feature. To set this up for use:

1 Open the Alexa app and access **Menu** > **Settings**

2 Tap on the **Voice Purchasing** button   Voice Purchasing

3 By default, the **Purchase by voice** option is On. Drag it to the Off position to disable voice purchasing

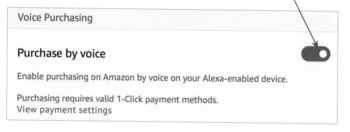

Voice Purchasing

Purchase by voice

Enable purchasing on Amazon by voice on your Alexa-enabled device.

Purchasing requires valid 1-Click payment methods.
View payment settings

4 Enter a four-digit code that will be needed to complete any voice purchases using Alexa on your Echo

Require voice code

Enter a 4-digit code that you'll say aloud when confirming your Amazon purchases. This spoken code appears in your history.

3791   SAVE CHANGES

5 Tap on the **Save Changes** button

Payment Options

In order for voice purchasing to work via your Echo, 1-Click purchasing has to be activated in your Amazon account. This can be done from the Amazon website and checked within the Alexa app:

1 Open the Alexa app and access **Menu** > **Settings**

2 Tap on the **Voice Purchasing** button | Voice Purchasing |

3 If 1-Click purchasing has been set up on

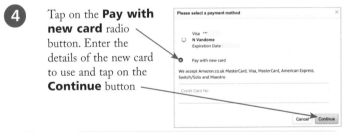

Payment Settings

All transactions are completed with 1-Click. Changes made to your default 1-Click method will apply to future Amazon.com 1-Click transactions, but will not change your current active subscriptions.

Your Default 1-Click Payment Method
Visa ending in | Edit Payment Method |

the Amazon website, details of the credit or debit card used for this are listed. Tap on the **Edit Payment Method** button to add a new card for using with 1-Click purchasing

4 Tap on the **Pay with new card** radio button. Enter the details of the new card to use and tap on the **Continue** button

Please select a payment method   ✕

◯ Visa ***
    N Vandome
    Expiration Date :

◉ Pay with new card

We accept Amazon.co.uk MasterCard, Visa, MasterCard, American Express, Switch/Solo and Maestro

Credit Card No

Cancel   Continue

Never give your voice purchasing passcode, created on the previous page, to anyone, unless you want them to make purchases on your card using voice purchasing.

Using Voice Purchasing

Once voice purchasing has been set up it can be used with Alexa in a number of ways to make and manage purchases on the Amazon website. However, you need to have an Amazon Prime membership (or free trial) to use voice purchasing on your Echo. Some options include:

- Buy new products from Amazon, by saying, "Alexa, shop for [product name]". If the item is available it will be added to your shopping cart and Alexa will ask if you want to buy the item. If the item is not available, Alexa will ask if you want it to be added to your basket or your Alexa shopping list. This includes items of food that can be found in the Amazon Pantry section of the Amazon website.

- Reorder items that have previously been bought, by saying, "Alexa, reorder [product name]".

- Buy music, by saying, "Alexa, shop for [song name], [album name], [artist name]". When an item has been identified, buy it by saying, "Alexa, buy [item name]".

- Track your current open orders, by saying, "Alexa, track my orders".

- Cancel an order, by saying, "Alexa, cancel order of [item name]". Orders should be canceled immediately after they have been made (or as soon as possible afterwards).

Beware

Voice purchasing only works with Amazon Prime-eligible products. There are currently no options for using other online retailers for voice purchasing.

8 Using Echo in the Home

Being able to control devices throughout the home, simply by issuing a voice command, is now very much possible and the Echo and Alexa are ideal for creating a smart home. This chapter looks at how you can communicate throughout the home using the Drop In feature. It then covers how to set up Alexa for using smart devices, and shows some of the devices that can be installed in the home and will interact with Alexa. These include smart lighting, which can be set up and used with a minimum of electrical expertise; smart heating; security options; and smart plugs for controlling electrical devices around the home.

Drop In

Within the home, the Echo is an excellent option for creating an internal intercom system. It is possible to communicate between Echos in different rooms in the home and also from the Alexa app to an Echo. This is known as Drop In. To use this:

1 On your smartphone, open the Alexa app and access **Menu** > **Settings** and tap on the **Echo** name

> **Nick's Echo**
> Online

2 Tap on the **Drop In** button (this can also be done when you first open the Alexa app on your smartphone, by tapping on the **Enable** button in the **Enable Drop In** window)

> **Drop In**
> Off

3 Tap on the option for who you would like to be able to use Drop In

4 Tap on this icon on the bottom toolbar of the Alexa app

5 Tap on this icon to add contacts for using Drop In

6 For the selected contact (including yourself, so that you can Drop In on the Echos within the home), drag the **Allow Drop In** button to On

7 Tap on the **OK** button to confirm access to Drop In

8 Tap on the button in Step 4 and tap on the **Drop In On [Echo name]**

9 Once the connection is made, you can communicate with the Echo in the same way as making a phone call. Drop In can also be used between Echo devices by saying, **"Alexa, drop in on [Echo name]"**, which is a great way to communicate between Echo devices throughout the home

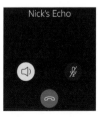

About the Smart Home

The idea of a smart home (i.e. one in which functions within the home can be controlled by computer devices) is no longer only within the realms of science fiction: it is very much a reality and within reach of everyone.

The Echo and Alexa can be put at the heart of a smart home, in terms of being able to control devices through voice commands; e.g. turning on the lights or adjusting the thermostat. Some of the types of devices that can be controlled with Alexa include:

- **Lighting**. Smart lighting systems can be installed, without the need for an electrician or electrical expertise, so that lights can be turned on and off with Alexa. They can also be dimmed and, with colored smart lighting sets, different color themes can be applied.

- **Heating**. Smart thermostats can be used to control central heating by changing the temperature or turning it on or off.

- **Locks and security systems**. Smart home security devices can also be controlled by Alexa to keep your property secure.

- **Sockets and plugs**. These can be controlled so that devices can be turned on and off around the home.

- **Curtains/Drapes**. Instead of having to open and close curtains/drapes manually, a smart system can be used to automatically close or open them when the appropriate command is made to Alexa.

- **A range of accessories** including air conditioners, humidifiers, fans and speakers.

Smart devices require access to a Wi-Fi network, and they can also be controlled with an appropriate app on a smartphone or tablet.

Adding Smart Home Skills

Smart home gadgets can be controlled with their own companion app, and relevant skills for a gadget can also be added to Alexa to make it possible for Alexa to communicate with the gadget. Most smart home gadgets have their own Alexa skill. To add smart home skills:

1 Open the Alexa app and access **Menu > Smart Home**

Smart Home

2 Tap on the **Your Smart Home Skills** button

YOUR SMART HOME SKILLS

3 Tap on the **Enable Smart Home Skills** button

ENABLE SMART HOME SKILLS

4 Tap on the required skill to add it to Alexa. This will act as a companion to the related smart home gadget. Without it, Alexa will not be able to communicate with the smart gadget

Most smart home devices will work with Alexa, but check with the technical specifications of the device to confirm this.

Adding Smart Home Gadgets

Once a smart home gadget has been set up, it can be added to Alexa so that it can be activated for voice control. To add a smart home gadget:

1 Open the Alexa app and access **Menu > Smart Home**

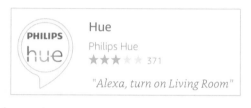

2 Navigate to the relevant smart home skill, as shown on page 83, and tap on it

PHILIPS
hue

Hue
Philips Hue
★★★★★ 371

"Alexa, turn on Living Room"

3 Tap on the **Enable** button to add the skill

PHILIPS
hue

Hue

Philips Hue

Rated: Guidance Suggested

★★★★★ 371

ENABLE

Account linking required

4 For some gadgets, you will have to register with the producer of the gadget. This can be done, for free, with an email address and a password. Once this has been done, tap on the **Yes** button to give Alexa permission to access the gadget

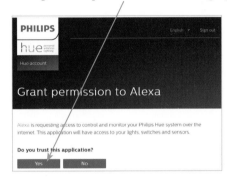

5 You will be notified if Alexa has successfully been linked with the gadget. Return to the Smart Home Homepage

...cont'd

6 On the Smart Home Homepage, under the **Devices** tab, tap on the **Add Device** button. The Alexa app will then look for any compatible Wi-Fi smart home devices that have been added (as shown on pages 84-85)

7 All of the items connected to the device are listed under the **Devices** tab. Tap on an item to view further details about it

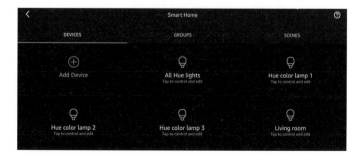

...cont'd

8 Tap on the Groups tab and tap on the **Add Group** button to control groups of smart home devices

9 Tap on a group name to view all of the available smart home devices that can be used here

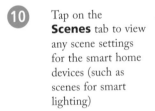

10 Tap on the **Scenes** tab to view any scene settings for the smart home devices (such as scenes for smart lighting)

11 Tap on one of the scenes to view details about it

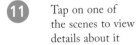

About Smart Lighting

Smart lighting is one of the most accessible and striking options for adding smart devices to the home: it can be set up in a matter of minutes, does not need an electrician (or any electrical knowledge) and creates a dramatic impact once it is up and running. Smart lighting also works impressively with Alexa.

Elements of smart lighting

The good news about a smart lighting system is that all of the components can be linked to existing elements of your home, and there is no need to alter any current equipment. Smart lighting works through a controller (bridge) that is connected to your Wi-Fi router, and the smart light bulbs are then controlled by Wi-Fi through the bridge. The elements required for a smart lighting system include:

- **Smart light bulbs**. These are light bulbs that can communicate using Wi-Fi via the smart lighting bridge. They can be either white, or white and colored, in which case they can change color and also create artistic scenes if more than one bulb is used in a particular room.

Smart light bulbs contain a considerable amount of technology and are more expensive than standard light bulbs. Single white bulbs are upwards of £10/$10.

...cont'd

- **Bridge**. This is the controller that is connected to your Wi-Fi router. Once it has been set up, this is where commands will be sent (either through a related app or a voice-control device, such as Alexa) and then distributed to the smart lighting system.

- **Remote control**. In addition to controlling the smart lighting through an app or a voice-controlled device, it can also be controlled with a remote control. This can be used to turn the lights on or off and dim them as required. If you have a group of smart lights in one room the remote control can usually only be used with the whole group, rather than controlling individual lights separately.

Hot tip

A good option for initially setting up a smart lighting system is to buy a starter pack. This will include a number of white or colored light bulbs, a bridge and a remote control.

Setting Up Smart Lighting

Smart lighting has a number of elements to it, and there are a few steps that have to be done before it can be used. (The examples here are for the popular Philips Hue smart lighting system, but the process is similar for most major smart lighting options.)

1 Insert the smart light bulbs and turn the lights on at the wall light switch and a lamp switch (if applicable)

2 Plug in the bridge and connect it to your Wi-Fi router using the supplied Ethernet cable

3 Download the related app, from either the Apple Store or the Google Play Store, to your smartphone or tablet

4 Open the app. It should locate the bridge automatically. Tap on the **Set up** button

Wi-Fi has to be working in order for smart home devices to work. If Wi-Fi is disabled, a device's app, or Alexa, will not be able to communicate with it.

5 Press the main button on the bridge to link it to the app

6 Tap on the **+** button to set up lights in specific rooms

7 Enter a name for the room (or use the default name already provided) and tap on the checkbox for the lights that you want to include in that room. Tap on the **Save** button to complete the room setup

Using Smart Lighting

Smart lighting can use white or colored light bulbs. The white ones are more functional and are best used in rooms where generally consistent lighting is used. White bulbs can still be dimmed through the app or by instructing Alexa, "Alexa, dim kitchen lights". However, it is with colored light bulbs that smart lighting really comes into its own. They can also be used as white bulbs, but it is best to think about them as color palettes that can be set to almost any color on the spectrum.

Companion apps can conduct a range of tasks in relation to the bulbs that they control. Some of them include:

1. Turn all of the lights on or off in a room

2. Turn individual lights in a room on or off

Hot tip

Each bulb is completely customizable individually and they can also be combined to create artistic scenes; see next page.

...cont'd

3 Select specific colors, or whites, for individual bulbs

4 Select preset color scenes, which set each bulb at an appropriate color and brightness

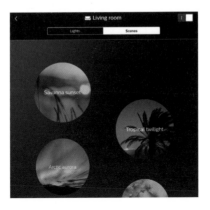

...cont'd

5 Create your own scenes based on an existing color setup, or a preset photo

6 Create a routine for your smart lighting, such as setting a time for the lights to come on, or go off, at specific times of the day or night

Alexa lighting commands

Once a smart lighting device has been added to the Alexa app, as shown on pages 84-87, Alexa can be used to control your lights, with some of these commands:

- "Alexa, turn [room name] lights on/off".

- "Alexa, dim/brighten [room name] lights".

- "Alexa, turn [room name] lights blue/green/orange etc.".

- "Alexa, turn on [scene name] in [room name]".

- "Alexa, turn [bulb name] on/off".

About Smart Heating

Smart heating systems enable you to control your central heating with a wireless thermostat that can be managed through a related app, or with Alexa (once the related skill has been added).

A smart thermostat should be fitted by a qualified installer (several devices have their own recommended installers), and once it has been set up and connected to your home Wi-Fi, it can be used to control and manage your central heating in a number of ways.

- Turn your heating on or off (either through an app or by using Alexa by saying, "Alexa, turn heating on/off").

- Set your smart thermostat to a specific temperature setting.

- Programme your smart thermostat to come on or go off at specific times. This can be as many times as you like during the day.

- Turn your heating on or off remotely (using the app).

- Control your hot water with complete flexibility.

- Apply a frost setting when you are away from home, if you are worried about pipes freezing.

Some smart thermostats can also learn from heating settings that you have used before. For instance, if you regularly have the temperature at the same level when you return home at a certain time, the smart thermostat will learn to set this automatically. They can also use sensors to determine whether you are home or not, and set the temperature accordingly. This helps to save energy, which is one of the main benefits of a smart thermostat.

About Smart Security

Smart home technology is an excellent way to add a range of security features to your home:

- Full security systems.

- Individual security cameras, for both external and internal use.

- Smart locks.

Full security systems

A full smart security system consists of a number of external cameras (usually three or more) that provide a live video feed of the exterior of your home. This can be viewed, via Wi-Fi, on a desktop computer, a laptop, a tablet or a smartphone. The cameras should have night vision capabilities and be weatherproof. Some systems can also record video to a hard drive, but these are more expensive. Alexa can be used with compatible systems  to instruct that a specific scene is displayed on the Echo Show (with video screen). External systems with a single camera, or a night light, are also available.

Not all full security systems are compatible with Alexa, so check this first before you invest in one of these systems.

...cont'd

Individual cameras

For security within the home, individual smart cameras can be used. This is most effective with Alexa and the Echo Show, so that the scene can be viewed on its video screen. This is an excellent option for parents who have babies sleeping in another room and want to be able to check on them.

Smart locks

Smart locks can be used with a range of options for unlocking and locking (including using Alexa, which usually has to be done with a hub that connects wirelessly to the lock, in a similar way as to controlling smart lights). The options include: key card; key tag; manual code; smartphone or tablet app; or Alexa. Do not rely solely on smart locks for a way to get into your home. Make sure that you have a manual alternative, in case any of the technology for the lock stops working. Alexa can be used within the home to give you peace of mind by locking all locks before you go to bed.

If there are other people in your home, let them know if you have a camera monitoring a certain room, so that they do not think you are spying on them.

About Smart Plugs

Smart plugs are a small but effective way of controlling electrical devices around the home. They are easy to set up, which can usually be done without the need of a separate hub or bridge connected to your Wi-Fi router. Some options for smart plugs include:

- Turning devices on or off.

- Creating timed schedules to turn devices on or off automatically.

- Checking the status of electronic devices, via the smart plug.

- Using remote access with a companion app.

Once smart plugs have been installed they can be paired to an Amazon Echo, by adding the relevant skill.

TP-LINK Kasa
TP-LINK
★★★½☆ 327

"Alexa, turn on the coffee maker"

Using smart plugs and Alexa is a great way to give yourself peace of mind at the end of the day, by using the instructions, "Alexa, turn off all plugs".

9 Trouble-shooting

The Echo and Alexa are usually pretty robust and efficient. However, there may be times when things do not always go exactly as planned or hoped. This chapter looks at some of the problems and issues that could arise when using an Echo and Alexa. It shows how to use Alexa itself and the Alexa app to identify problems and seek solutions. It also covers issues to do with connecting to an Echo and various sound problems that can arise.

Asking Alexa for Help

Things rarely go smoothly all of the time with any computing device. There will probably be times when your Echo doesn't work as expected, or doesn't work at all. For the former, Alexa is a good starting point for trying to find out the problem. To do this:

1   Ask Alexa a query, such as, "Alexa, how do I change the wake word?"

2   For some questions, such as in Step 1, Alexa will provide the answer. The answer will also be shown on the Homepage of the Alexa app

> ### How do I change the wake word?
> To update the wake word, go to the Settings section of the Alexa app. Select a device, and then Wake Word.
>
> More ⌄

3   If Alexa does not have an immediate answer you will directed to the **Help & Feedback** section of the Alexa app. Open the Alexa app. A Help panel is displayed at the top of the page. Tap on the **Things To Try** button to view some of the options within the Help & Feedback section. Tap on the **More** button to view the exact question that has previously been asked

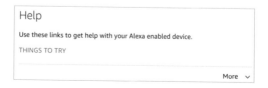

> ### Help
> Use these links to get help with your Alexa enabled device.
> THINGS TO TRY
>
> More ⌄

Using Help & Feedback

Within the Alexa app there is a comprehensive Help & Feedback section, covering a range of issues that can arise with the Echo and also Alexa. To use this:

1 Open the Alexa app and access **Menu > Help & Feedback**

Help & Feedback

2 Under the **User Guide** section, tap on one of the main Help categories to view the sub-categories within it

3 Navigate through the sub-categories until you find the required topic. Tap on the topic to view the full details

4 Under the **Contact Us** section, tap on the required links to contact Customer Service, or send feedback

Connection Issues

Even after an Echo has been set up and is working properly, there may still be times when there are connection issues, either with your home Wi-Fi or a Bluetooth connection for an external device. Some of the issues that may occur, and possible solutions, are:

● **Alexa does not respond when you issue an instruction**. This could be due to a faulty power connection. Check the Echo plug at the wall socket and ensure it is turned on. Also, check the cable to ensure it is not damaged, or has been pulled loose from the Echo at any time; e.g. when furniture is being moved around.

● **The Echo does not connect to your home Wi-Fi network**. Initially, check if the issue is with the Wi-Fi router or with your Echo. To do this, check on another device to see if it can connect to the Wi-Fi router in the usual way. If it is an issue just with the Echo, there are a number of troubleshooting options to try: move the Echo nearer to the router to see if the issue was being too far away to pick up a strong signal; reset the router and try connecting the Echo again; or, check in the Wi-Fi settings of the Alexa app (**Menu** > **Settings** > **[Echo name]** > **Update Wi-Fi**).

● **The Echo does not connect to an external Bluetooth device**. Make sure the device itself is in pairing mode so that the Echo can find it. In the Alexa app, go to **Menu** > **Settings** > **Bluetooth** and tap on the **Pair a New Device** button. If the device is still not recognized, move it closer to the Echo and retry.

Check on the web to see if your Bluetooth device is compatible with the Echo. More devices are being added on a regular basis, so if it is not compatible, it may be soon.

Sound Issues

Generally, if you treat your Echo well, there will not be too many problems with the sound. However, there are some issues that could arise and they include:

- **There is no sound from the Echo**. Check that the volume has not been turned down with the decrease volume button on the top of the Echo. Press the increase volume button to see if this fixes the problem. If there is still no volume, it could be as a result of the speakers not working. This can be solved by replacing the subwoofers and tweeters in the speaker, although it could be cheaper to replace the whole Echo.

- **Sounds for alarms, timers or notifications cannot be heard**. Check in the sounds settings of the Alexa app (**Menu > Settings > [Echo name] > Sounds**) to make sure that the appropriate volumes are turned up sufficiently and have not been muted.

If you play music too loudly on your Echo this could blow the speakers, or damage them so that the sound becomes distorted.

...cont'd

- **Alexa has problems recognizing your voice commands**. Make sure that the Echo is in a good location: away from walls; not on the floor; and clear of any devices that could cause interference, such as microwave ovens or baby monitors. After giving a command, check what Alexa heard, on the Homepage of the Alexa app. Tap on the **More** button to see exactly what Alexa heard. Tap on the **Learn more** button to view additional options.

- **Alexa cannot hear you at all**. Check that the microphone on the Echo has not been turned off. This is done by pressing the microphone button on top of the Echo. If the microphone is off, the button and the light 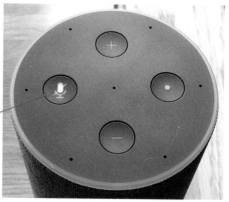 ring at the top of the Echo turn red. Press the microphone button to turn it back on, so that Alexa can hear you. (This can also be used to specifically mute the Echo, so that Alexa will not hear any commands, made either deliberately or accidentally.)

Hot tip

There are regular software updates for the Echo and Alexa, and these could fix some connection and sound issues. These are usually installed automatically over Wi-Fi.